PIANO ★ VOCAL ★ GUITAR

contemporary COUNTRY

ISBN 0-634-01594-X

HAL•LEONARD® CORPORATION

7777 W. BLUEMOUND RD. P.O. BOX 13819 MILWAUKEE, WI 53213

Visit Hal Leonard Online at
www.halleonard.com

CONTENTS

AMAZED

Words and Music by MARV GREEN,
CHRIS LINDSEY, and AIMEE MAYO

Moderately slow Country Ballad

*Recorded a half step lower.

1. ba-by, I'm a - mazed by you.

2. ba-by, I'm a - mazed by you.

Ev-'ry lit-tle thing that you do.

I'm so in love with you. It just keeps get-tin' bet - ter.

THE BEACHES OF CHEYENNE

Words and Music by BRYAN KENNEDY,
GARTH BROOKS and DAN ROBERTS

D.S. al Coda

CODA

enne.

No - bod - y can ex - plain ___ it. Some say she's still a - live. ___

They e - ven claim they've seen ___ her on the

shore - line late at night. So, if you go down by the

BETTER MAN, BETTER OFF

Words and Music by BRETT JONES
and STAN PAUL DAVIS

I'm gon - na

BLUE

Words and Music by
BILL MACK

A BROKEN WING

Words and Music by SAM HOGIN,
PHIL BARNHART and JAMES HOUSE

She loved him like he was ___ the last man on earth.

Gave him ev-'ry-thing she ev-er had.

Original key: B major. This edition has been transposed up one half-step to be more playable.

With a _____ bro - ken wing, _____ she _____ car - ries her dreams.

Man, you ought to see her fly.

COME CRYIN' TO ME

Words and Music by WALLY WILSON,
JOHN RICH and MARK D. SANDERS

COWBOY TAKE ME AWAY

Words and Music by MARTIE SEIDEL
and MARCUS HUMMON

Original key: F# major. This edition has been transposed up one half-step to be more playable.

DRINK, SWEAR, STEAL & LIE

Words and Music by MICHAEL PETERSON
and PAULA CARPENTER

I was twelve when dad-dy said to me, _____
Last night I threw a-way my twelve-step book. _____

"Don't take to drink-in', boy, that road don't lead no where. _____
I fin-'lly faced the fact that I am hooked on you. _____

And don't you ev-er let me hear you swear. _____ Don't you
There's noth-in' more that I can do. _____ Ain't no

EVERYTHING'S CHANGED

Words and Music by PAUL NELSON,
LARRY BOONE and RICHIE McDONALD

Yeah, ev-'ry-thing's _ changed _ ex - cept for the way _ I feel a-

bout _ you.

Repeat and Fade

Optional Ending

FOR A LITTLE WHILE

Words and Music by PHIL VASSAR,
STEVE MANDILE and JERRY VANDIVER

Moderately

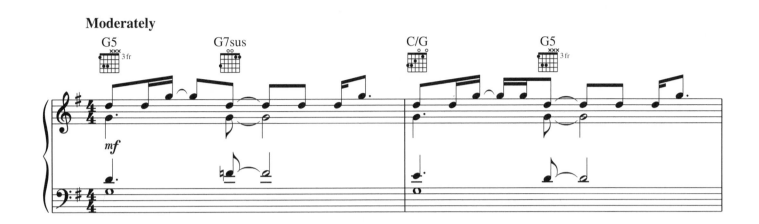

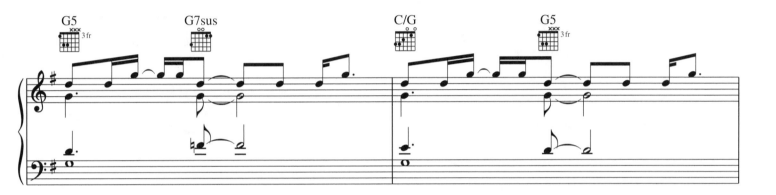

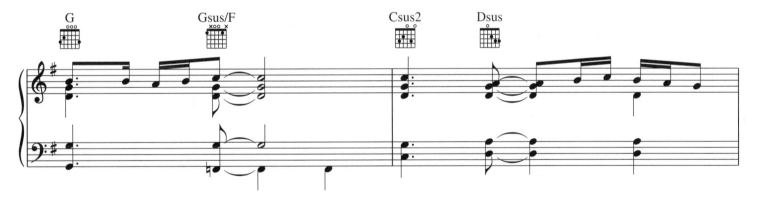

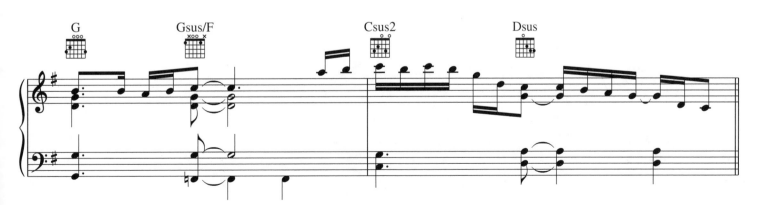

left me with __ a smile, __ for she was mine for a lit-tle while. __

We take a ride __ and head on down to Air - port Road. __

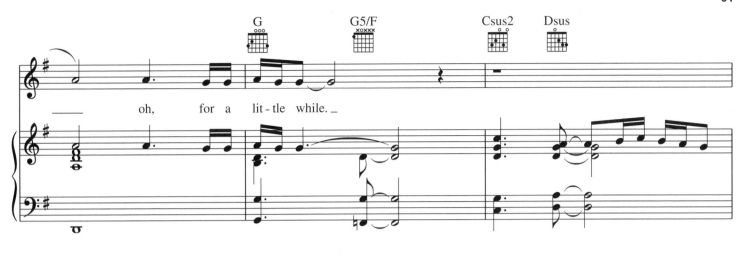

oh, for a lit - tle while. _____

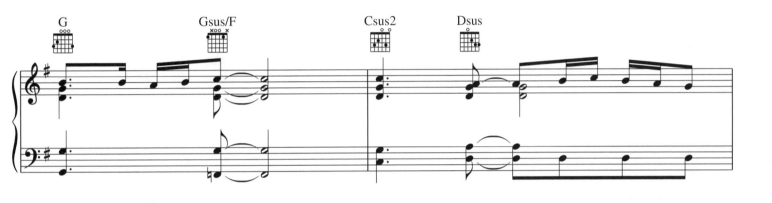

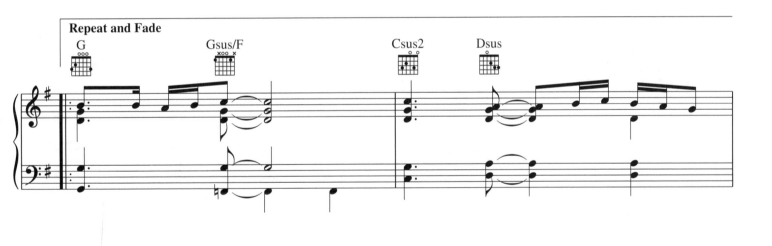

Repeat and Fade

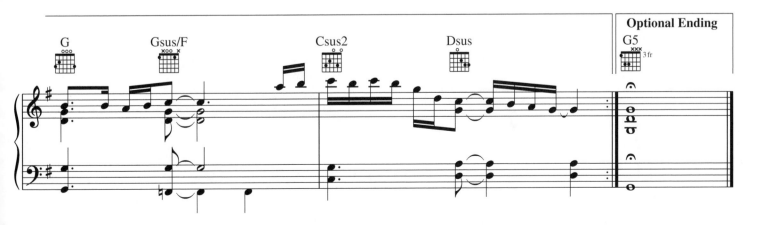

FROM HERE TO ETERNITY

Words and Music by ROBERT ELLIS ORRALL
and MICHAEL PETERSON

HE DIDN'T HAVE TO BE

Words and Music by KELLEY LOVELACE
and BRAD PAISLEY

HOW DO I GET THERE

Words and Music by DEANA CARTER
and CHRIS FARREN

We've al - ways been the best of friends, ___
You prob - 'ly think I've lost my mind, ___

HOW LONG GONE

Words and Music by JOHN SCOTT SHERRILL
and SHAWN CAMP

HOW YOUR LOVE MAKES ME FEEL

Words and Music by MAX T. BARNES
and TREY BRUCE

I'm no po-

HUSBANDS AND WIVES

Words and Music by
ROGER MILLER

I CAN STILL FEEL YOU

Words and Music by TAMMY HYLER
and KIM TRIBBLE

You said you ___ feel you. _____

I JUST WANT TO DANCE WITH YOU

Words and Music by ROGER COOK
and JOHN PRINE

I don't want to be the kind to
caught you look-in' at me when I

hes-i-tate ___ and be too shy, ___ way too late. ___
looked at you. ___ Yes, I did. ___ Now ain't that true? ___

I don't care what they say oth-er lov-ers do, ___ I ___
You won't get em-bar-rassed by the things I do, ___ I ___

I'M ALRIGHT

Words and Music by
PHIL VASSAR

I LOVE YOU

Words and Music by TAMMY HYLER,
KEITH FOLLESE and ADRIENNE FOLLESE

I'LL THINK OF A REASON LATER

Words and Music by TIM NICHOLS
and TONY MARTIN

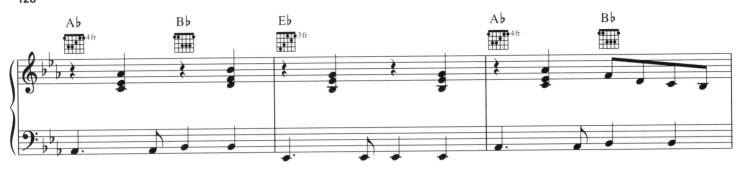

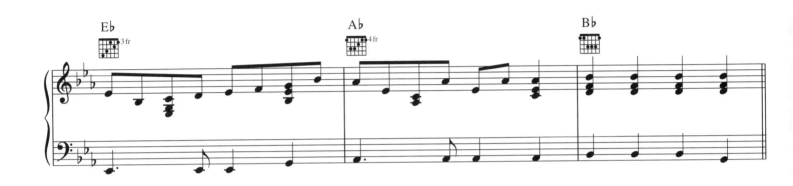

In - side her head _ may _ lay _ all the an - swers for cur - in' dis - eas - es from bald -

- ness to can - cer. Salt of the earth _ and a real _ good danc - er, but I _

I'M SO HAPPY I CAN'T STOP CRYING

Written and Composed by
G.M. SUMNER

The park is full of Sun - day fa - thers and melt - ed ice _ cream. _ We try to do the best _ with - in _ the giv - en time. A kid should

IT MATTERS TO ME

Words and Music by ED HILL
and MARK D. SANDERS

IF YOU SEE HIM/IF YOU SEE HER

Words and Music by JENNIFER KIMBALL,
TOMMY LEE JAMES and TERRY McBRIDE

Moderately

A LESSON IN LEAVIN'

Words and Music by BRENT MAHER
and RANDY GOODRUM

LONGNECK BOTTLE

Words and Music by RICK CARNES
and STEVE WARINER

A LITTLE PAST LITTLE ROCK

Words and Music by TONY LANE,
BRETT JONES and JESS BROWN

LITTLE RED RODEO

Words and Music by PHIL VASSAR,
CHARLIE BLACK and RORY MICHAEL BOURKE

LONELY TOO LONG

Words and Music by BILL RICE,
MARY SHARON RICE and MIKE LAWLER

LOVE OF MY LIFE

Words and Music by KEITH STEGALL
and DAN HILL

came and saved me from _ my-self. Now all ___ I real-ly know is I

need ___ you.

You are ___ the love of my life. ___

You are ___ the rea-son I'm _ a-live. ___

A MAN THIS LONELY

Words and Music by RONNIE DUNN
and TOMMY LEE JAMES

ONE NIGHT AT A TIME

Words and Music by ROGER COOK,
EDDIE KILGALLON and EARL BUD LEE

I'm not yours, and ba-by, you're not mine. _

MY BEST FRIEND

Words and Music by AIMEE MAYO
and BILL LUTHER

NO PLACE THAT FAR

Words and Music by SARA EVANS,
TOM SHAPIRO and TONY MARTIN

PLEASE REMEMBER ME

Words and Music by RODNEY CROWELL
and WILL JENNINGS

Original key: D♭ major. This edition has been transposed down one half-step to be more playable.

mem - ber me.

Re - mem - ber me when you're out walk - ing,

when snow falls high out - side your door,

late at night ___ when you're not sleep - in'

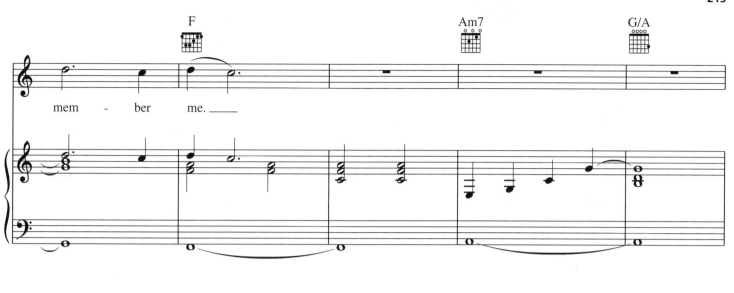

mem - ber me. ___

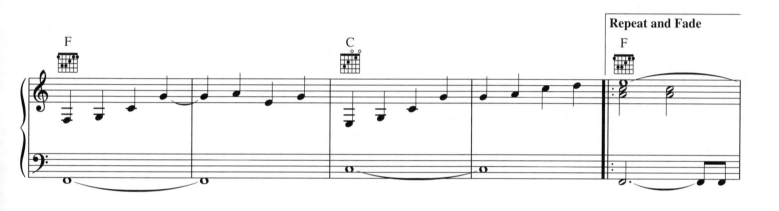

Repeat and Fade

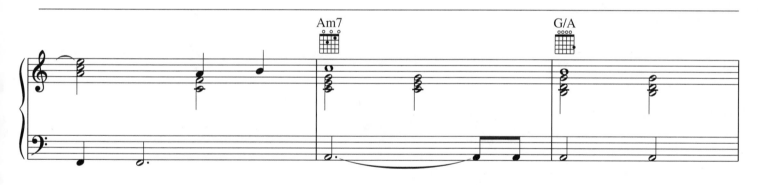

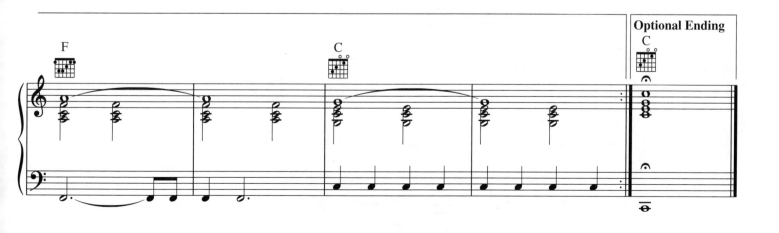

Optional Ending

READY TO RUN

Words and Music by MARTIE SEIDEL
and MARCUS HUMMON

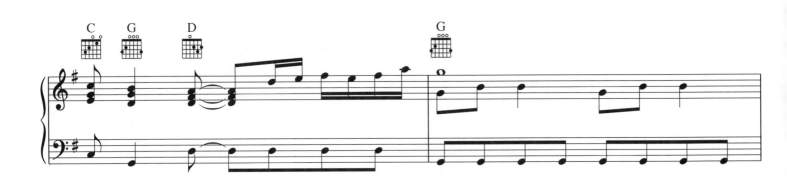

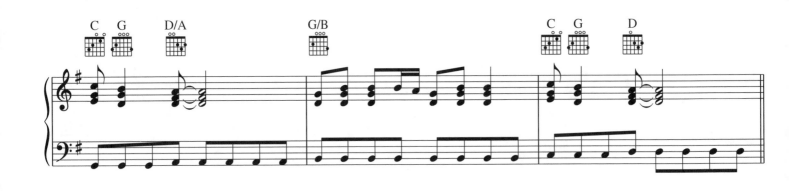

SHE THINKS MY TRACTOR'S SEXY

Words and Music by JIM COLLINS
and PAUL OVERSTREET

Moderately fast

Plow-in' these fields in the
ride ___ back and forth till we

hot sum-mer sun ___ and o-ver by the gate, lord-y, here she comes ___ with a
run out of light. ___ Take it to the barn, put it up for the night. _____

N.C.

Repeat and Fade

Optional Ending

RIGHT ON THE MONEY

Words and Music by CHARLIE BLACK
and PHIL VASSAR

SHE'S GONNA MAKE IT

Words and Music by KENT BLAZY,
KIM WILLIAMS and GARTH BROOKS

SINGLE WHITE FEMALE

Words and Music by SHAYE SMITH
and CAROLYN DAWN JOHNSON

Original key: G♭ major. This edition has been transposed up one half-step to be more playable.

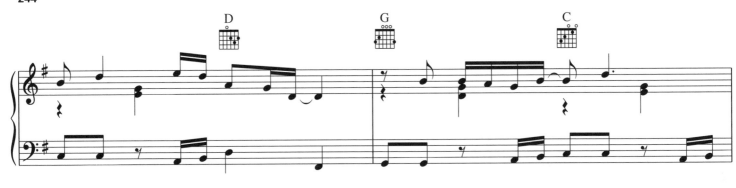

It's my con-fes - sion, I hope you get the mes - sage ___ that there's a

like you. I'm look-in' for a man ___

245

THANK GOD FOR BELIEVERS

Words and Music by MARK ALAN SPRINGER,
ROGER SPRINGER and TIM JOHNSON

Last night I came home a-gain,
She says, "Boy, I still love you."

three sheets to the wind. ____ Broke the prom-ise I swore I'd nev-er break.
She's strong-er than the nine-ty proof ____ I've sent cours-in' through my veins.

THERE YOU HAVE IT

Words and Music by RICK GILES
and STEVE BOGARD

You're the kind of wom-an   I've been dream-in' of, ___   but I nev-er thought _

that I could ev-er say it good   e-nough ___   to

252

(This Ain't)
NO THINKIN' THING

Words and Music by TIM NICHOLS
and MARK D. SANDERS

Moderately

I've been think-in' 'bout our love ___ sit-u-a-tion, ___
For-get ___ math-e-mat-i-cal e-qua-tions, ___

all this at-trac-tion in the pres-ent tense. ___ I've reached the on-ly log-i-
self-help psy-chol-o-gy. ___ Grey mat-ter don't mat-

WIDE OPEN SPACES

Words and Music by
SUSAN GIBSON

Who does-n't know what I'm talk-ing a-bout?

WHERE THE GREEN GRASS GROWS

Words and Music by JESS LEARY
and CRAIG WISEMAN

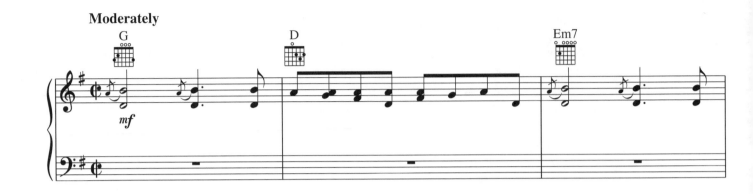

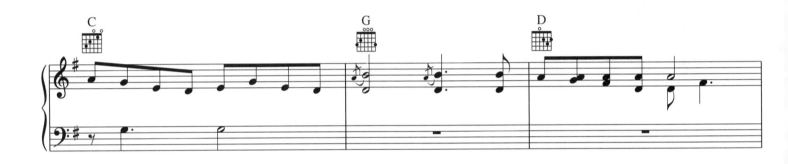

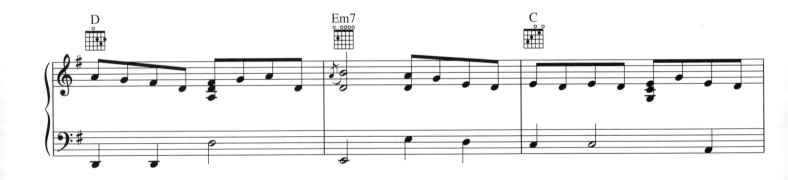

whoa, _____ where the green grass grows. _____

YOU HAD ME FROM HELLO

Words and Music by SKIP EWING
and KENNY CHESNEY

YOU WERE MINE

Written by MARTIE SEIDEL
and EMILY ERWIN

YOU'RE BEGINNING TO GET TO ME

Words and Music by AARON BARKER
and TOM SHAPIRO

YOU'RE EASY ON THE EYES

Words and Music by TERRI CLARK,
CHRIS WATERS and TOM SHAPIRO

eyes, hard ___ on the heart. ___

Contemporary & Classic Country

More great country hits from Hal Leonard arranged for piano and voice with guitar chords.

#1 Country Hits of the Nineties – 2nd Edition

The second edition of this great compilation includes 26 hits: Achy Breaky Heart • Boot Scootin' Boogie • Chattahoochee • Check Yes or No • Friend in Low Places • Longneck Bottle • Love Without End, Amen • My Maria • She Is His Only Need • Wide Open Spaces • You're Still the One • more.
00311699......................................$12.95

51 Country Standards

A collection of 51 of country's biggest hits, including: (Hey Won't You Play) Another Somebody Done Somebody Wrong Song • By the Time I Get to Phoenix • Could I Have This Dance • Daddy Sang Bass • Forever and Ever, Amen • God Bless the U.S.A. • Green Green Grass of Home • Islands in the Stream • King of the Road • Little Green Apples • Lucille • Mammas Don't Let Your Babies Grow Up to Be Cowboys • Ruby Don't Take Your Love to Town • Stand by Me • Through the Years • Your Cheatin' Heart.
00359517......................................$14.95

100 Most Wanted

Highlights: A Boy Named Sue • Break It to Me Gently • Crying My Heart out over You • Heartbroke • I.O.U. • I Know a Heartache When I See One • Mammas Don't Let Your Babies Grow Up to Be Cowboys • My Heroes Have Always Been Cowboys • Stand by Me • Save the Last Dance for Me • You're the First Time I've Thought About Leaving • You're the Reason God Made Oklahoma • many more.
00360730......................................$15.95

90's Country Gold

29 chartburners, including: Achy Breaky Heart • Boot Scootin' Boogie • Down at the Twist and Shout • Friends in Low Places • I Feel Lucky • Neon Moon • Shameless • She Is His Only Need • Straight Tequila Night • and more.
00311607......................................$12.95

Hot Country Dancin'

Over 30 toe-tapping, boot-scootin' favorites guaranteed to get you dancing! Includes: Achy Breaky Heart • Friends in Low Places • Here's a Quarter (Call Someone Who Cares) • Hey, Good Lookin' • I Feel Lucky • and more.
00311621.................$12.95

The Award-Winning Songs of the Country Music Association – 1984-1996

40 country award-winners, including: Achy Breaky Heart • Ain't That Lonely Yet • Baby's Got Her Blue Jeans On • Boot Scootin' Boogie • Daddy's Hands • Down at the Twist and Shout • Forever and Ever, Amen • Friends in Low Places • God Bless the U.S.A. • I Swear • The Keeper of the Stars • Where've You Been • and more. Also includes a photo library of the winners.
00313081......................................$17.95

Top Country Hits of '98 - '99

23 chart-topping country tunes: How Long Gone • Husbands and Wives • I Can Still Feel You • I Just Want to Dance with You • A Little Past Little Rock • Right on the Money • That Don't Impress Me Much • There You Have It • Wide Open Spaces • Wrong Again • You're Easy on the Eyes • You're Still the One • more.
00310489......................................$12.95

Country Love Songs

34 songs featuring: Butterfly Kisses • Check Yes or No • For the Good Times • I Never Knew Love • Love Can Build a Bridge • The Vows Go Unbroken (Always True to You) • and more.

00311528......................................$12.95

Country Inspiration

21 sentimental favorites, including: Brotherly Love • Guardian Angels • I Saw the Light • Love Can Build a Bridge • Love Without End, Amen • The Vows Go Unbroken • Why Me Lord? • and more.
00311616.................$10.95

Good Ol' Country

58 old-time favorites: Candy Kisses • Cold, Cold Heart • Crazy • Crying in the Chapel • Deep in the Heart of Texas • Faded Love • Green Green Grass of Home • Hey, Good Lookin' • I Can't Stop Loving You • Sweet Dreams • Tennessee Waltz • You Are My Sunshine • You Don't Know Me • more.
00310517......................................$14.95

The Best Contemporary Country Ballads

30 heart-felt hits, including: After All This Time • Alibis • The Greatest Man I Never Knew • I Can Love You like That • I Meant Every Word He Said • I Want to Be Loved like That • If Tomorrow Never Comes • One Boy, One Girl • When You Say Nothing at All • Where've You Been • more.
00310116......................................$14.95

Today's Women of Country

Includes 24 hits by top artists such as LeAnn Rimes, Reba McEntire, Faith Hill, Pam Tillis, Trisha Yearwood and others. Songs include: Blue • Down at the Twist and Shout • The Greatest Man I Never Knew • I Feel Lucky • Mi Vida Loca (My Crazy Life) • When You Say Nothing at All • more!
00310446......................................$12.95

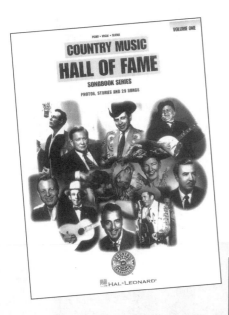

The Country Music Hall Of Fame was founded in 1961 by the Country Music Association (CMA). Each year, new members are elected – and these books are the first to represent all of its members with photos, biographies and music selections related to each individual. Each edition is arranged for piano, voice and guitar.

COUNTRY MUSIC HALL OF FAME
SONGBOOK SERIES

Volume 1

Features Jimmie Davis, Tennessee Ernie Ford, Minnie Pearl, Jim Reeves, Hank Williams, and others. Over 25 songs, including: The Ballad Of Davy Crockett • Can The Circle Be Unbroken • Deep In The Heart Of Texas • Jambalaya (On The Bayou) • May The Bird Of Paradise Fly Up Your Nose • Mule Train • Rocky Top • You Are My Sunshine • Your Cheatin' Heart • and more.
00313058...$12.95

Volume 2

Features Roy Acuff, Owen Bradley, Lester Flatt and Earl Scruggs, Tex Ritter, Merle Travis, Bob Wills, and more. Over 25 songs, including: Divorce Me C.O.D. • He Stopped Loving Her Today • I'm Sorry • San Antonio Rose • Sixteen Tons • Wabash Cannon Ball • and more.
00313059...$12.95

Volume 3

Features Gene Autry, Johnny Cash, Roy Horton, Bill Monroe, Willie Nelson, Frances Preston, Ernest Tubb, and other Hall Of Famers. Songs include: Always On My Mind • Folsom Prison Blues • I Never Promised You A Rose Garden • It Makes No Difference Now • Kentucky Waltz • On The Road Again • Ring Of Fire • Sugarfoot Rag • Tennessee Saturday Night • Tumbling Tumbleweeds • Walking The Floor Over You • and more.
00313060...$12.95

Volume 4

Features Eddy Arnold, Chet Atkins, the Original Carter Family, Merle Haggard, Pee Wee King, Hubert Long, Roger Miller, Floyd Tillman, and more. Over 30 songs, including: Bouquet Of Roses • Dang Me • Green Green Grass Of Home • Happy Trails • Heartbreak Hotel • If You've Got The Money (I've Got The Time) • John Henry • King Of The Road • Mama Tried • Okie From Muskogee • Tennessee Waltz • Yakety Axe • and more.
00313061...$12.95

Volume 5

Over 30 songs from Hall Of Famers such as Patsy Cline, Jim Denny, Connie B. Gay, Loretta Lynn, Marty Robbins, and others. Songs include: Blue Eyes Crying In The Rain • Coal Miner's Daughter • Crazy • 'Deed I Do • El Paso • I Fall To Pieces • The Long Black Veil • Pistol Packin' Mama • Ruby, Don't Take Your Love To Town • You Ain't Woman Enough • and more.
00313062...$12.95

FOR MORE INFORMATION, SEE YOUR LOCAL MUSIC DEALER, OR WRITE TO:

HAL•LEONARD®
CORPORATION
7777 W. BLUEMOUND RD. P.O. BOX 13819 MILWAUKEE, WI 53213

Visit Hal Leonard on the internet at http://halleonard.com

Prices, contents and availability subject to change without notice. Some products may not be available outside the U.S.A.